MAKING MAGIC

Intentional Moments for Educating Young Children

MANUEL KICHI WONG

Making Magic: Intentional Moments for Educating Young Children
Copyright © 2018 by Manuel Kichi Wong

tellwell

Tellwell Talent
www.tellwell.ca

ISBN
978-0-2288-0096-5 (Hardcover)
978-0-2288-0095-8 (Paperback)
978-0-2288-0097-2 (eBook)

TABLE OF CONTENTS

INTRODUCTION

Working with children, teachers, parents and colleagues has brought much joy and satisfaction to my life. I thrive on the fast-paced life of a teacher; I get to observe constant changes in emotional development in children as they learn to use words to describe how they are feeling, play and interact with new friends. I get to watch as they develop their language by singing songs, acquire new skills—from hopping to hand coordination—and, through writing, begin letter recognition of their names.

After hundreds of hours over 35 years dedicated to choosing a life's work in the human service field, I've learned a lot and about how my heart feels about children and come to many conclusions about the role of being a teacher in their lives. I have found that life is exciting when I, too, can include compassion, positivity and respect in my daily interactions and practices with children, and doing so gives me the strength to carry on such important work. I've learned how to be more understanding of children through my "intention-based" teaching style where I focus on being involved in the moment while I am in the classroom, as well as taking the time to learn more about them from their parents. The end result is that I am happy—truly filled with happiness—and motivated to give more and reflect on changing my teaching strategies to meet the individual child.

Over the years I have observed so many new teachers and parents seeking more guidance in working with children. Past and present students have asked me "What do I do if I get hired as a teacher after taking the four foundation classes (Orientation to Early Childhood Education, Early Childhood Curriculum, Child Growth & Development, and Child, Family & Community)?" Hopefully this book will help guide them. And for those currently working with children, this may be a refresher of teacher choices they forgot or didn't learn in school.

My educational experiences began at City College, where I took general education classes before transferring to San Francisco State University to major in Social Welfare. This was years later when I began taking classes in Early Childhood Education (ECE) and then obtained my Masters in the ECE program. I have an abundance of experiences that I am thankful for through my background running a family child care with six children, to working with up to a hundred children in large center both by being a teacher and a director of typically developing children and children with disabilities. I am happy to share and pass on what I have learned, and still experience on a daily basis, to be of value in my classroom setting.

From my perspective, *Making Magic: Intentional Moments for Educating Young Children* is an overview about the choices we make today with how we feel, what we say and do, and how we live our life being about *choice* instead of *chance*. It's our choices in deciding to feel, see, smell, touch, dream, wish and give that make us all unique. Working with children is not a random path as we have all made the choice to do this with our lives. And the choices we make each day can make a huge difference in how we can best equip children with tools of independence, self-control, with making good choices, with self-esteem, and a positive way of seeing the world. So, you see, the "randomness" of thoughts starts with you. You alone can write or print your own action plan for your life and, in turn, enrich the lives of the children you interact with each day.

I coined the term "Teacher Choice" many years ago while teaching classes in early childhood curriculum. Teachers and parents make choices each and every day for themselves and what they do in the classroom or a home environment.

In this book I'd like to share my "Twenty Top Teacher Choices," practices I live by in the classroom. Of course, there are many hundreds of practices that teachers can add, but these are the most essential ones I practice on a daily basis. I hope that by using these Teacher Choices you find your day with children brings you joy, and the children experience and learn to value their uniqueness, sense of wonder, and a childhood filled with surprises of comfort and learning.

For every Choice I have also included some "random thoughts." These are meant to help spark an appreciation of children in your care, and I suggest you add your own about the children you work with or have in the space provided on each page. Your own observations and thoughts that you write can be a jumping off point of knowing the children you work with better. When you know children better, you are able to form relationships where you can understand them better. This can lead to you providing care, materials and experiences that will guide the child onward to higher learning, self-satisfaction, being motivated and happy children each and every day.

On the adjacent page, I've listed my "random" thoughts about how I see children in hopes that they might spark joy and appreciation. I have seen that when people have an appreciation of children, they act, talk and interact differently and with more intentionality, helping to form positive connections with their students or parents with their own young children.

Feel free to write your thoughts in the space provided at the bottom of each page. Think of this area as a journal of the children you work with so that you can reflect, change or add experiences to always keep a positive momentum going each and every day. Motivation comes from being happy with life, people you are around, and, for many working in the field, a deep satisfaction of gratitude and honor being around children. Enjoy your daily journey working with children; every day I've learned that I, too, learn with every interaction.

I dedicate this book to Rosemary Kennedy, a true advocate for children, parents and teachers. She was my true mentor in motivating me, and in giving me more courage to stand up for children and make this world better for the families we serve in the San Francisco Bay Area. Rosemary was instrumental in advocating for family child care providers, for wage incentives, for teacher assistants, and established funds for family child care support groups. Rosemary will be truly missed (July 2017) by all of us who knew her. In her memory please get involved in your community to support teachers, families and children.

My good friend and longest early childhood educator colleague of 30 years, Kerri Dukas (September 2017), will also be missed for her long-standing gift of giving to the children as a teacher. I learned that caring deeply and practicing high standards of appropriate practices with children leads to excellence.

From both my friends, I have learned that living is giving and that each moment counts. I pass on my book to you so you too can contribute to the lives of children and families each day of your life.

Manuel Kichi Wong
January 2018

TEACHER CHOICE 1:

Prepare to be a teacher.

Be prepared by taking educational classes related to children and having some direct child-related experiences. Teachers make choices each day to be a positive influence while working with children. They must have a good education based in developmentally-appropriate practices that include knowing what children need at their current age of development. This means choosing furniture, toys, and play experiences that meet individual developmental needs of each child; this includes having appropriate materials that include cultural images of the children (books that might be bilingual, pictures current of families at the school, baby dolls from many cultures).

Teachers also have to be flexible enough to attend to the changing needs of each child while at the same time be consistent and predictable with daily routines and schedules. An example of this is when "Charlie" is painting a picture and it's clean up time and he is not finished. A teacher can give Charlie a little more time to finish or even the option of finishing up the picture later on that day. This shows flexibility and also respecting Charlie and his work.

Getting yourself together also means physically and mentally. Physically might mean that you have a good breakfast, you have brought your own lunch with good protein, fruit and good carbs. You have a plan in knowing what you will do with the children each day by writing down daily activities on your planning sheet, getting materials needed ahead of time (like the book you might want to read, special art materials for collage), and have a plan in case it rains for movement inside instead of outside.

To be mentally prepared includes some examples I already gave, but also how might you handle: spilled milk for the second time on the floor; wet pants to change; a sick child who vomits on the rug; children fighting over a toy and one gets hit on her lip and it bleeds; children running around the classroom; or children who won't go to sleep. How mentally prepared with strategies are you in knowing what to do in supporting children in their time of need? You must know how to deal with crying children who miss their parents, know the art of patience and be calm in the classroom when four or five children need your attention. Are you ready for any unforeseen situations that might happen during the day? Being receptive, happy, thoughtful and in good humor can also be good traits to have at these times.

Random thoughts:

- A child is like a pair of glasses with eyes that focus on what children are doing at the moment.

- A child is like a piece of glass: so fragile, yet so strong.

- A child is strong, determined and unique.

- A child is like a thank you for being with you.

WRITE YOUR THOUGHTS HERE:

TEACHER CHOICE 2:

Greet every child and family member with a smile that's authentic.

Getting down to the child's eye level is a way of showing respect, so we can see their faces, and make contact. At this greeting we are doing many things. A morning health check consists of looking at the child's face, eyes and, sometimes, touching the face to feel their temperature. We are establishing a warm presence and a happy voice that says "Good morning" and "I'm glad you here." We ask questions to the children about their sleep, what they ate, or inquire about a scratch or what happened if they have a Band-Aid on. All these questions help us to gauge how the child is feeling so, in some cases, we might adjust their day to meet their needs.

For example, a child says she did not eat breakfast; I might tell them we have cereal and apples in the kitchen to eat if they'd like. If they tell me they are tired, then I might suggest they go get a book or find a cozy area if they need a rest. When a child feels comfortable about their teacher and thereby experience at school, it helps them in many ways, especially with the transition from home to school. If a child is feeling sad, teachers need to address the situation and reassure them by offering assistance with warm support. Taking feelings seriously can either make or break a child's day at school.

All these positive interactions also help the parent or guardian feel comfortable. If the parent is comfortable and confident that their child is being well taken care of, they show this in their goodbyes to their child with their smiles. If a parent is not comfortable or appears stressed out, the child feels this and might have a harder time saying goodbye. This is our cue as teachers to give support to a crying child and give comforting words to the parent such as "I will be with Sally and help her ease into school today."

Since the parents know their child the best, teachers can learn from the parents in understanding the child at home and this can be useful with our interactions with the child at school. At the beginning or end of each day, some children and parents might need help to come into school or to leave. This is our cue to support parents and children at this time. A good welcome makes it a good day for everyone and a good, happy "See you tomorrow!" helps with a goodbye. Important transitions at school help children and parents cope with separation better and help children develop consistent and predictable routines.

Random thoughts:

- A child's emotions change from happy to sad with a snap of two fingers.

- A child's goodbye can be teary-eye sad.

- A child is like a rainbow of colors with beauty.

- A child is like reading a book with unexpected challenges each minute in school.

WRITE YOUR THOUGHTS HERE:

_____

_____

_____

_____

_____

_____

_____

_____

_____

_____

_____

_____

_____

_____

_____

_____

_____

TEACHER CHOICE 3:

Model appropriate behaviors.

Children are like the lambs from the song "Mary Had a Little Lamb," they are impressionable in many ways, from infancy to early childhood age and beyond. It's amazing how children follow many of the leads and actions of those they see around them, from grandma spreading jam on her toast to dad dipping his sushi in soy sauce.

As teachers you have the responsibility to model good practices, from what you say to the tone of your voice, how fast you talk, and how you speak with children. If you are demanding, loud and disrespectful to children, the children will copy as you do. Teachers in each classroom set the tone for being examples. Classroom teachers who practice respect, compassion, good listening skills, practice problem solving skills with sharing toys, model cleaning up and being helpful with one another, help children to learn these skills and practice them daily. Children develop habits or etiquette by practicing what they see and hear such as: "Excuse me," "Thank you," "Can I help you?" and waiting till the person stops speaking.

Random thoughts:

- A child is like a circle that goes around and around.

- A child is like a microphone that experiments with voice.

- A child is like a flag blowing in the wind.

- A child is like a dream, he wakes up and his world is his to conquer.

WRITE YOUR THOUGHTS HERE:

_____

_____

_____

_____

_____

_____

_____

_____

_____

_____

_____

_____

_____

_____

_____

_____

_____

_____

Teacher Choice 4:

Remember: you have a choice in being happily involved with children.

Happy teachers are seen as motivated individuals that care for children and strive to help them meet their needs each day. Being happy is contagious and children need this for a good beginning of their education.

Teachers should have a genuine interest and excitement in working with children and participating in the activities children choose each day. Most recently I have seen a teacher sit near children while they work together building an elaborate structure of a two feet high house with the magnetic shapes. The teacher did not interrupt the play but just sit nearby and from time to time commented on what she was seeing. She did not guide the play by telling the children what to do or tell them that if they put that piece there, the structure would fall. She let the children work together to problem solve the mishap of part of the house falling down and let them figure out what to do. Letting children do for themselves does equal happy children because they are not told what to do. This type of creative play is meaningful and satisfying which leads to creating self-esteem and builds community among the children. When teachers can appreciate through observation and letting children make their own choices in play, they are witnessing emerging skills of motivation and learning driven by the children. These are all skills we want to support each day for all our students.

Random thoughts:

- A child guides their own play moment by moment.

- A child is like a million emotions all mixed up.

- A child is like a capital "I": Important, Impressive and Innocent.

- A child is like a shooting star, firing off sparks of comments and thoughts.

WRITE YOUR THOUGHTS HERE:

_____

_____

_____

_____

_____

_____

_____

_____

_____

_____

_____

_____

_____

_____

_____

_____

TEACHER CHOICE 5:

Create routines and a balanced schedule.

For children, daily schedules are parts of the day that stay the same. It's like a timeline that children follow; schedules are consistent so children know what they will be doing each time of the day. Knowing what happens next helps children feel secure, gives them choices of what type of play is offered, and gives them some control in their school life.

A typical morning schedule:

1. Greeting by a teacher
2. Hang up jacket
3. Eat breakfast or snack
4. Free choice of activities for an hour
5. Small group experiences with the same teacher (art, music, reading books)
6. Outdoor time for one hour
7. Lunch
8. Nap time

The schedule is repeated after nap with the added element of going home.

Children learn routines during the day when they wash hands, clean up toys, brush their teeth and put their shoes on. Teachers support children throughout the day to complete the elements of the schedule and guide those who need support during routines. Children become independent through the experience of practicing routines and this helps them at home too. The skills learned at school are also life skills for daily life activities and organization of time.

Random thoughts:

- A child can do what adults can't do without being seen as funny.

- A child's feet move one way, the eyes other way, and bang right into a child and cries.

- A child is like a key in the ignition that keeps on running, even when the engine is turned off.

- A child is like a crystal, always sparking.

WRITE YOUR THOUGHTS HERE:

_____

_____

_____

_____

_____

_____

_____

_____

_____

_____

_____

_____

_____

_____

_____

_____

_____

Teacher Choice 6:

Establish a community feeling during meal times.

Sitting with children at meals times builds community with the students and strengthens the relationships among peers and the teacher. This time together builds language and social skills, while also offering an introduction to different foods they might not experience at home.

Conversation skills are taught by repeated experiences with adult role models and children with some of the same skill attributes. You are a role model; how and how fast you eat can show children ways to be safe, especially not talking while eating food. Memories around eating are created by listening and participating in conversations during meal times and are life skills that all children should be exposed to. Make meal times a positive and relaxing experience, where they can all share the moments of the day while learning table etiquette.

Children are encouraged to eat but do we not force children to eat. If a child says "No" to a food, do not place the food on the child's plate. "Family-style eating" is a practice that some schools use so children can pass the plate or bowl around the table and help themselves. This gives a child the ability to take a serving of food they want or not.

Random thoughts:

- A child is like an inflated balloon being blown up.

- A child is like a marker who, when it's about to dry out, always has a little more color to give.

- A child is like a familiar song: the tune is the same but the words might be different.

- A child is like reading a good book with a happy ending.

WRITE YOUR THOUGHTS HERE:

_____

_____

_____

_____

_____

_____

_____

_____

_____

_____

_____

_____

_____

_____

_____

_____

TEACHER CHOICE 7:

Create play spaces for children.

A comfortable environment that is child-centered are spaces that have appropriate furniture that are suitable for that age group and have a distinct separate area of play.

Creating spaces for children is important as this is where they play each day. A well-designed play space offers choices, places to be alone, has materials for independent and group play, and is key in learning all basic skills for school life (social, emotional, cognitive [thinking skills/problem solving], fine motor [hand coordination] and gross motor [movement, dancing, running, jumping, and climbing] that can be seen in the outdoor environment).

A rule of thumb is that the table is waist-high and chairs are low enough for the child's feet to touch the floor. Play areas are divided by shelving and carpets to delineate specific learning areas, such as the book, writing, art and science areas, distinguished from the small toys, blocks and house areas.

Most classrooms will have a block area separated by shelving with the house area on the other side. The block area for three-year old's will have wood blocks, cars, diverse family people,

Duplo, animals and a train set. The house areas—sometimes called the "dramatic play area"—will have: a play stove, refrigerator, sink, table and chairs for at least four children, food items and dress-up clothes. A nice, solid, low pile carpet will help determine the space for the block area as this adds comfort to children who are playing on the floor.

In both areas here, the toys will be labeled on the shelves, kept in baskets or clear containers with the picture of the item and in some cases the word of the item on each container. You might see a container of cars with a picture of cars and the word car on the container. This helps children put back the toys back in their appropriate place for easy clean up.

Creating spaces for children that are divided in areas help children concentrate on that one type of play and, at the same time, helps children learn self-regulation, which is how they act and play in each area—like how to behave in a library opposed to playing ball outside. You will see children in both in the house and block area be more active, verbal, and expressive. You will see them playing individually or in small groups. Other areas will tell children how to act and change their play dramatically. If a child were in the writing or book area, he/she will be sitting down, their voices might be softer and they will have different tools (pencils, markers and paper for the writing area) than in the house area. Self-regulation is a skill worth developing in early childhood programs for future skills needed in different environments.

Random thoughts:

- A child is like the keys on a piano with both high and low notes of emotions.

- A child is like a green tree who, when watered with daily care, will thrive and grow.

- A child is like the rain, when the tears come, they don't stop.

- A child is like a soft bear, it can be squeezed but bounces right back.

WRITE YOUR THOUGHTS HERE:

Teacher Choice 8:

Include home-like items in the classroom.

Bringing familiar home-like items into the classroom helps children build a connection between home and school. Being around familiar objects can also help children in their play. Encourage teachers or children to bring items, toys and materials such as: measuring cups, child-size pots, pans, plates, hats, scarves, clothes, empty food containers such as cereal boxes—items that will have meaning because they are also seen at home. Other home-like items could be cultural items: a tortilla press, Chinese child-size wok, or plastic foods such as bread, fruit and vegetables. Larger items might include a carpet from India, small pillows for the couch from Mexico, a calendar from another country with photos, and musical instruments from other places. In this way a cultural aspect can be added to the classroom

Random thoughts:

- A child is like two dancing feet, tapping in time to the music, like a heartbeat.

- A child plays with enjoyment and learning.

- A child sees what's important right now with what he/she is doing at the moment.

- A child is like a scream that echo's loud feeling.

WRITE YOUR THOUGHTS HERE:

_____

_____

_____

_____

_____

_____

_____

_____

_____

_____

_____

_____

_____

_____

_____

_____

_____

Teacher Choice 9:

Read to children every day.

A love of books starts from those who provide a place that is cozy with softness, books that include culture, diversity, children and favorite familiar objects, and stories of interest about feeling and life.

Offer children reading opportunities inside and outside the classroom. This could be when you have a few children in the early morning or when some children are waking up for nap and you have the opportunity to create a small reading time with your primary group outside. Make it a part of your daily schedule and let children choose the books they want you to read. A love of reading comes from a literacy-rich environment that includes: hearing words, having conversations, writing, drama, singing and writing experiences for children.

You will notice that some children like the same books read every day. If you're wondering why, one theory is that children feel comfort and joy at times when they know the story. As stories become familiar to them, they start to know what comes next and many can participate by pointing to pictures as you read. This is how new words are learned by pointing to a picture, an adult or the child naming it, and it goes on from one word to many in a matter of months.

Enjoy the togetherness of reading. It's a bonding time that reinforces shared interest and togetherness. We want our children to have a love of books and, as we know now, early reading experiences help children in writing skills too. When teachers write the words (called dictation) with children, this also lets the children know that their words are important. Children begin to recognize the connection between the written word and the spoken work. This is so true when children recognize their name written and then see the same letters somewhere in the classroom environment. A love of reading comes when children participate, have books of interest available, and through your show of excitement in reading and telling stories.

Random thoughts:

- A child is like a dictionary with words that increase with exposure.

- A child is an ever-changing thought.

- A child is a "tip toe" on hardwood floor trying to avoid the squeaking of the floor boards.

- A child is rambling words that go on and on and on.

WRITE YOUR THOUGHTS HERE:

_____

_____

_____

_____

_____

_____

_____

_____

_____

_____

_____

_____

_____

_____

_____

_____

_____

_____

_____

_____

TEACHER CHOICE 10:

Create a safe and comfortable environment.

Supervision is key. You can anticipate that children will hurt themselves if the environment is not safe, so do your daily safety checks of the indoor and outdoor areas before children play and get rid of any hazards. These could be things like: standing water, broken toys, branches on the ground for the outside and inside, small items that might cause choking on the floor, loose carpets, unstable chairs and shelving that has become loose from the walls.

Your role as a teacher is to keep children safe always. However, getting physically hurt happens most days as children will fall down, bang into each other while running, slip on the stairs while walking or get bitten by another child. In all these instances, the child will need to be looked at and the teacher should determine what type of first-aid should be given.

All of these require three steps:

- help the child immediately with one-to-one attention,
- give some type of aid to heal the hurt,
- document the incident for the parent and school.

Psychological comfort is meaningful and goes a long way in helping children build relationships. Sometimes it's just a good hug and kind words of understanding to the hurt body area. Sometimes it's an ice pack on a finger that's hurt even if you don't see any physical signs of hurt. (It's the psychological aspect of caring that helps children feel better.)

Random thoughts:

- A child cries for his or her parents at any time of the day.

- A child claps and jumps with joy when they are happy.

- A child whispers in your ear, the special moments of importance, for only you to hear.

- A child is like a ball of yarn adding yardage with each positive moment.

WRITE YOUR THOUGHTS HERE:

_____

_____

_____

_____

_____

_____

_____

_____

_____

_____

_____

_____

_____

_____

_____

_____

Teacher Choice 11:

Provide a clean school environment with healthy practices.

Cleaning the school environment is part of our role as teachers; this is mainly seen in wiping surfaces and hand washing. Teachers can miss simple health and safety requirements because of limitations in time, supervision in the restroom area and rapid scheduling, but it is vital to help reduce the spread of germs.

Tables have to be washed many times including: before the arrival of children in the am; before and after eating food; any diapering areas and hand washing sinks. Hand washing occurs: before and after eating; when hands get messy from sticky play; before and after playing with playdough; when using water play; before and after touching animals or insects; after restroom or body fluids from the body; before and after coming to school or from outside activities.

Your role is to help guide children to wash their hands in the above examples using proper procedures.

Proper hand washing procedure is:

1. Ensure two minutes of hand washing to include wetting hands
2. Rub soap on all parts of the hand
3. Turn off faucet with paper towel
4. Dispose of the paper towel in a hands-free step garbage can

RANDOM THOUGHTS:

- A child seeks challenges so unique to that child.

- A child is like a rainbow with each color so different and exuberant with power.

- A child dreams happy thought when adults respond with respect.

- A child snuggles up like a cat in bed and reaches for your hand to lick you.

WRITE YOUR THOUGHTS HERE:

_____

_____

_____

_____

_____

_____

_____

_____

_____

_____

_____

_____

_____

_____

_____

_____

Teacher Choice 12:

Engage children through interesting toys and hands-on experiences.

Hands-on experiences are important for developing fine motor skills and problem-solving techniques; toys can help children learn both of these skills by using their hands and figuring out the toys they play with. Give children time to explore at their own pace but at the same time support those who become frustrated with care and attention.

You will see children playing with many of the same toys daily, or others who go many times from one toy to the next. The younger the child, the more you may see them tasting and biting toys; infants and young toddlers learn through their senses and need that oral sensation. Times when a new tooth is coming in are signs where children will just about pick up any toy to put in their mouth. If safe, let them enjoy it, and then wash it after they put it down. (Warm water, rinse with clean water, and put gently into a sanitizing solution with water and bleach. See recommendations on the web.)

Using your observation skills, you will be able to see when a child can do a five-piece puzzle. You should also have other puzzles with more pieces that offer greater challenges. Remember that all children develop skills at different times, so it's your role to support children where they are at the moment. You may see some children playing with toys for younger children, but's that's ok. Repeated experiences build competencies that move to higher-level learning.

Random thoughts:

- A child is like two colors mixing in a puddle of paint.

- A child is like an airplane soaring high.

- A child is like an open mouth with expression.

- A child is like a train, always making life connections.

WRITE YOUR THOUGHTS HERE:

TEACHER CHOICE 13:

Provide sensory, creative and "free choice" activities every day.

In every classroom there is a time in the morning and afternoon for "free choice time." Free choice time is when children are able to select areas of the classroom to play in.

One area should be art, which is also a sensory area. In the art area, you could have playdough, clay, sand, water, bins of corks or smooth pebbles for touching or filling cups. The art area should have open-ended materials to create three-dimensional art. You will need cardboard, form and cereal boxes for the foundation. From there you will provide glue and masking tape so children can build whatever they want. This is called "open-ended" art because children can create whatever they want. No two creations children make will be the same, each is unique and individually made. You could also provide the children with materials such as: scraps of construction paper, popsicle sticks, corks, fabric pieces, empty jewelry boxes, paper towel insert and Styrofoam from packaging. Remember to supervise and use materials that are compatible to the ages of the children, small items might be a choking hazard.

In terms of children who have never painted, I'll include a few guidelines:

Prepare the tables with newspaper to cover the table. If children are new to painting, you might give them some direction of using the paintbrush (don't be surprised if children use their hands or fingers). Be prepared with paper towels for cleaning hands and have the sensory area/paint area near a sink for easy clean up. I suggest four children at time in this area and, if possible, sit with the children as they enjoy table experiences.

If you setup playdough or clay experiences, you can set up identical tools (plastic pizza cutter, wood rolling pin, tongue depressors and small cupcake molds). Many teachers set up play experiences for four children because it's manageable and you can give more individual attention to this small group of children. Talk with children and help them problem solve when challenges arise with the materials. Introduce words such as "small," "large," and "snake-like" when using playdough. When making open-ended art, describe what you see, have children talk about what they made. At the end of these activities, help children participate in clean up. Remember *not to make, draw, or do art for children.* Let the children do it for themselves and experience any experience at their own rate. Give guidance and supervise when needed, especially if a child is eating materials (playdough) and let them know it's for touching only.

Random thoughts:

- A child learns gentleness with each breath he/she takes.

- A child is like salmon swimming up against the current.

- A child is like a spinning top running in circles.

- A child is a bounty of sunshine when the weather calls for hail.

WRITE YOUR THOUGHTS HERE:

_____

_____

_____

_____

_____

_____

_____

_____

_____

_____

_____

_____

_____

_____

_____

_____

_____

Teacher Choice 14:

Offer new elements of sensory play.

Invite the children to experience something out of the ordinary. This could be: play with water; play with sand; play with sound; play with clay; play with homemade Gak made with cornstarch and water; play with rocks tumbling through tubes into water; play with different kinds of textures to make sounds; play with bubbles; play with PVC tubes outside that build up and fall down; play with fabric pillows; play with vocal sounds made on from the body; and just play with ice, slushy jello, or finger paint.

Remember to set up the environment safely: do it at the right place (water play on washable floors with a mop available for spills) or even outside where the mess doesn't have to be contained like the indoor environment. Start and end the activity with the children involved in helping to clean up. It could as simple as putting their smocks on a hook, wiping the spill up with a paper towel, or, for older two-year old's using small brooms to sweep up the sand on the ground. All these experiences help build a community of helpers that promotes independence and care for the environment.

Random thoughts:

- A child is like a bird flying high to touch the sky.

- A child is like a kiss, thoughtful hand reaches to the lips to an outward motion to say goodbye.

- A child is like the wheels on a bus, always turning.

- A child is about music and music is me. La, La, La…

WRITE YOUR THOUGHTS HERE:

_____

_____

_____

_____

_____

_____

_____

_____

_____

_____

_____

_____

_____

_____

_____

_____

_____

_____

TEACHER CHOICE 15:

Encourage individual creativity whenever you can.

Art and creative experiences are all so messy, experiential, personal, unique, individual and so "open," meaning there is "no wrong way" to use the materials. There are guidelines, however, in using the materials (pencils, clay, glue, watercolor, markers, chalk, easel painting, water and food coloring, tape, fabric, sting, tissue paper and construction paper) so they are safe and do not break. Markers for examples can be broken if they are fist pounded on the table. So, teachers can show the proper use of them. Once learned, children can experiment with colors any way they like. Other creative outlets might include musical instruments and singing. Children can create music any way they like and familiar songs with different words. This shows creativity and uniqueness, and should be encouraged.

Random thoughts:

- A child is like a wake-up smile.

- A child is like a yellow balloon that goes pop with surprise.

- A child is like a guitar strumming cords, changing, with beauty and sound.

- A child's day only happens once. Tomorrow is different. Enjoy the moment.

WRITE YOUR THOUGHTS HERE:

Teacher Choice 16:

Get children outside to play.

Children need to have time every day to run, jump, climb, slide, catch bubbles in the air (gross motor experiences), play with water and sand, sing, dance, read books, play with art, build with blocks, ride bikes, chase flies/butterflies and generally be out in nature.

Remember the supervision aspect of children outdoors and strive for children to play only on age-appropriate play structures, swings and equipment. Practice guidance rules, and interact and remind the children on the many safety aspects of outdoor play. For example: going down the slide one child at a time; only one child going up the ladder; only three children on the tire swing at a time. Always give a rationale to children such as, "I am here to keep you safe so no one gets hurt."

Having a garden helps teach them about growing things, watering and, if it's a vegetable, an edible learning process that might encourage trying different foods.

Fresh air, trees, blue sky and birds offer new ways of seeing the world. A play structure with a slide, climbing ladders, crawling tunnels with a safe rubberized ground covering will make the outdoor area safer. All schools are required to have outdoor experiences in the morning and afternoon, so you can make it a place that children can enjoy.

RANDOM THOUGHTS:

- A child is sunshine on a strong rainy day.

- A child plays with imagination differently each and every moment in play.

- A child is our gift to support like a floating cloud.

- A child is like a crack on the road with beauty.

WRITE YOUR THOUGHTS HERE:

Teacher Choice 17:

Explore your school neighborhood.

Getting out in the community offers children opportunities to explore one's neighborhood. It offers children times to touch and smell the flowers, look up into the sky and ask perplexing questions about the "why" of the sky and where the birds go when it rains. It's an opportunity to talk about what they see, feel, smell and wish. These are the times to investigate the world beyond the classroom and bring it back into the classroom with memories of children drawing of what they see, questions they pose about birds, the truck they see, the new building, the types of dogs they encounter and the changing of seasons.

As a teacher you can extend the children's learning back into the classroom by investigating their observations. A very popular way of doing this is doing a project about a specific topic of interest. An example of this would be when children ask, "What kind of bird is that and where does it live?" While on your outdoor walk, take pictures of the bird; from there you go to the library—by yourself or with the children—and get books about birds. From there you see what type of bird you saw; from there the children might draw what their bird might look like; from their children might make bird houses; from there you might makes outdoor housed for your school yard to attract birds. This whole process starting from the interest of a child is a learning experience, and in the process, you are supporting their skills—from drawing, imagination, hands-on work, language, introducing new words—and at the same time encouraging children to build enthusiasm for learning.

This process is a time to create shared experiences that are memorable, valuable and meaningful. Children learn best when they choose activities and pursue an interest by investigating and taking about what's important to them. Children also bond with their peers when they have similar interests and thus form friendships which support self-esteem and a sense of belonging. By extending learning to outside the classroom, you, as a teacher, can give the children purpose to the projects they learn inside and show them the connection to the outside world.

Of course, your other role outside the classroom on walks is to keep the children safe. Address safety rules such as: walk in twos; stop at corners and wait for directions from the teacher; one teacher leads the children with one teacher at the back of the group. Take time to have conversations during your time outside, they are so meaningful to children, especially if you talk about what interest them.

Random thoughts:

- A child is like a form-fitting sock.

- A child is like a tear drop, dropping slowly to the sound of one's own breath.

- A child is like a conversation, give and take, and give and talk.

- A child is deep with knowing, feeling, and determination.

WRITE YOUR THOUGHTS HERE:

Teacher Choice 18:

Be attentive to the changing needs of children.

Giving individual attention at the right time feels monumental for many teachers in the classroom. Some typical classrooms of three to five-year old's have up to 24 children with three teachers. With so many children with individual needs to address (children arguing over a toy, a child hits another child, toileting care, crying children over not having a friend or missing a parent, children running inside), a teacher could start running in circles trying to meet them all. Your body presence, calm nature in addressing the situation, and your verbal and caring words to children can be a start. Address any situation in this manner and take steps to help the needs the child may have at the moment. At any of these times I have mentioned, you are assisting children in some type of change of action, address feelings of sadness, or helping them problem solve. Some examples of this might be when a child runs in the classroom. Focus on the behavior you want such as "Walking feet keep you safe."

Children who are crying for a parent need calmness, compassion and the use of words, something like "I know you miss

Mommy. Let's talk about it." The teacher might repeat what the child says and then add at what time the parent will be coming back in a way the child can understand, for instance "after lunchtime." Always address the feeling of the child missing the parent and, in time, hold the child's hand. In some cases, the child may want to be carried. Take cues from the child slowly and take your time.

Other situations where you can give one-to-one attention to a child can be: reading stories together or in small groups; during daily hand washing; during child-choice free play at tables where children are doing activities; when children come up and share a picture they did or shout out "Look what I made with the blocks!" would be your introduction to interact.

Remember to get down to the child's level and verbally and even non-verbally let the child know you are interested. Don't be like a giraffe talking down to children but at the same level. Being nearby also creates physical space that lends to give support and may result with teachable moments such as a question or comment from a teacher to a child.

Random thoughts:

- A child may like to share his or her ideas. Listen and respond.

- A child is like a giggle, silenced squeezed into a thundered Boom!

- A child is like a smile who lights the moon on a story night.

- A child is like a basketball cap, you can cover the head but the eyes speak under the brim.

WRITE YOUR THOUGHTS HERE:

_____

_____

_____

_____

_____

_____

_____

_____

_____

_____

_____

_____

_____

_____

_____

_____

TEACHER CHOICE 19:

Observe children and document results.

Observing students is key for any teacher working in a class-room, especially those working with children. Teachers can learn about individual skills (language development, color and number recognition, physical abilities, cognitive/problem solving, fine motor skills, and creative abilities in the arts) which is important so teachers can form a learning plan for each child. Learn about the children's' skills and what areas of development a child might need support in through observing and documenting it on paper.

For example: the use of scissors. Many three-years old's might not be able to use scissors because of their lack of experience or lack of fine motor control. In terms of cutting and using scissors, the hands have a high level of dexterity, hand control and strength. Observation is key in determining if the child has skills in this area and this leads the teacher into giving appropriate support with the use of scissors. If the teacher recognizes that the child has limited experiences with fine motor activities, she/he might offer playdough, ripping up paper, and puzzles with knobs to get the child's hands stronger. With these experiences and one-on-one assistance children will learn to use the scissors, but this will take time.

Observation helps us determine what materials to put out on the shelves that are developmentally appropriate for the child. Key concepts for teachers would be: observe, see the skill level of each child, select or remove toys that are too challenging but at the same time offer some challenges to those children who can complete an eight-piece puzzle, and have a few with 10 to twelve-piece puzzles to increase their competency with puzzles.

Communicating with parents can help form positive connections with the family and the child. Spend some time each day observing each child so you can respond to questions from families about the child's progress. Use a notebook with a page (or more) for each child and note down what you see. You can share this with parents and they will be reassured you are paying attention to their child. Both you and the parents can learn how to support the child through these observations and share in the growth and development of the child. What you do in the classroom benefits all children, especially when you have planned activities and experiences where each individual child can grow and develop.

Random thoughts:

- A child seeks a peaceful happy heart and contentment in play and relationships.

- A child dreams of being older to do what he cannot do right now.

- A child wonders if adults were once children and if they wished they could stay children forever.

- A child is creation with each passing day - a star.

WRITE YOUR THOUGHTS HERE:

_____

_____

_____

_____

_____

_____

_____

_____

_____

_____

_____

_____

_____

_____

_____

_____

TEACHER CHOICE 20:

Lesson Plans help ensure quality standards.

Teachers need to have a documented written daily plan working with children each day. This would include all areas of development that include experiences in all areas of development such as: reading times for listening to stories and introducing vocabulary, materials for math and science experiences for problem solving, art experiences for creativity, dramatic play for pretending and developing social/emotional development and outdoor time for gross motor and building large muscles. The intent of planning the day would be for the benefit of the students and individually meeting early childhood standards. Beginning with the teacher doing individual assessments and observations of each child, the teacher will learn where the child is developmentally in all areas of development. An example might be that Betty has a hard time communicating with other children as shown by her hitting children when she wants a toy someone else has. The teacher's awareness of this can help Betty be more competent by providing experiences such as reading books on how to take turn and providing experiences daily for Betty and other children to build competencies in this area. In the teacher's lesson plan, she/he will be intentional in providing these experiences, see how these teaching strategies work or not work, thus, supporting Betty in meeting her individual goals. Another daily lesson play might be to include sensory experiences that might include clay or play dough play. Through the teacher's observations saw that many children did not know how to properly hold a scissor and saw in the classroom that there was not enough fine motor experiences and the teacher knew that children first had to have many experiences to build up the hand control before holding scissors or writing with pencils. So, the lesson plan will include daily experiences so children can strengthen more control for competencies through every day experiences.

RANDOM THOUGHTS:

- A child uses her hands as tools of discovery.

- A child moves towards friendship for seconds at a time.

- A child creates thoughts like no one else.

- A child is like a red heart always pumping blood with energy.

WRITE YOUR THOUGHTS HERE:

Today is November 12, 2017. I'm sitting here at the Vancouver Public Library, overlooking the sounds of children and their parents playing, looking at books and older children shuffling through the shelves to find a book to read. How I chose to be in this place to write my book, *Making Magic: Intentional Moments for Educating Young Children*, is not by accident but by choice. There is magic here at the library as people explore books, do research, learn about new ideas, and concentrate on interests that fill up moments in their lives. That's how I see my time with children. Time to give magical moments of experiences that fill up their time, but are also valuable for their current life to build upon experiences, for now and the future. Teachers help create experiences in early childhood that help contribute to a child's wellbeing, this helps them begin the process of learning about themselves and the world around them. We create learning spaces that include top-down learning from their brains to their feet. Our early childhood education classes are geared toward providing teachers with information to meet the many needs of children in our care; it's like a recipe or prescription of how and what we will provide for children.

I hope you will read and use my Top 20 Teacher Choices daily in your care of young children. All of them can be used either at home or a school setting to help guide children with experiences that will foster growth and development to enhance their brains, move their bodies and give them the hands-on experiences they need at the beginning of their young lives. I hope my suggestions for Teacher Choices will give those beginning teacher's new ways of being with children or, as I've said earlier, *refresh* skills not readily practiced.

You, as educators, can create magical experiences with your classroom environment. With your positive attitude and own imagination, you can create an openness to try new things. See children as true individuals with capabilities to gain a good sense of self, abilities to create play on their own, find meaning by learning from peers, and, most importantly, find life exciting. In this way you will help them be a thinker of ideas and find a feeling that helps make one's self happy.

These Teacher Choices are professional practices and foundational elements of curating the right learning environment. There are so many that you, yourself, will develop, and I encourage you to write these down even after you finish this book. Think of this book as an ongoing chapter in your continuity of learning. I have found that even after my many years of experience, each day brings more learning. With an open mind and the ability to see many other views, I have become a richer and more understanding person. I do not *know it all* as I learn each moment, like the children. This is the magical part of being human. Enjoy the journey.

CLOSING THOUGHTS

Let each day be joyful, exciting, full of learning, respectful, thankful and, as I tell my students, "Have a good life." Being a teacher or a parent has many responsibilities because the lives of the children we are with are influenced by our interactions.

A caring adult at the right time with young children can give solitude, guidance and understanding in our fast-paced world. The choices that adults make with children can have positive effects and, in the future, you may find the child looking back at you saying, "You were there for me, and I'm glad you made the right choices for a caring school or home."

Teachers are one of the primary influences with the growing children. Students can be either "turned on" or "turned off" learning. I've seen this happen when some teachers do not know how to talk with students respectfully, encourage and motivate them, set up classrooms that can guide students in positive ways of growing intellectually, value each student for their uniqueness, and support students who are struggling to form relationships with peers or gain an excitement in learning. On the positive side, teachers can be encouraging, thoughtful listeners, and guides—both educationally and as a self-worth supporter. As role models and examples for our children, we help support and guide them each and every moment they are with us. Even when we are not physically there, children carry with them the experiences, feelings, attitudes, and skills of being able to cope in life.

This is not a role to take lightly, so a question you might ask yourself before taking it on is: Am I the best person I can be to support the many needs of children in the classroom physically, emotionally, heart of giving (spirit), and go the extra yard each and every moment in the classroom to show students "a way of being" that can be respected in the world?

How did you do in writing your thoughts about the Teacher Choices you read about? Are you, or will you be, practicing them in your everyday interactions with students? Can you see the benefits made upon the students and yourself as well? Have you been able to extend your care of students to a higher level? Have you been able to "see the light bulb" go off in your head to move on to a more fulfilling career or life? Will you make a more conscious effort in caring for children in a way that shows gratitude, satisfaction, and joyfulness each and every moment? Have you been able to see that your actions can influence each and every person you interact with each day?

Making the "right choices" can change the world of the students we work with. It's up to you, and I hope that your gift of giving will be truly authentic. We have so much to give and so little time. As I've said to my college students, "Children only go around once, give them the best, understand and grow, and in the end, be pleased with what you have given to yourself and your community."

Enjoy life, as life is not random, as we choose our own destiny and leave our earthly footprints in the lives of the children who have walked in our path. Pass on what you have learned and share your new reflections as a start of a new beginning. Energize each moment with the children to find more ways to appreciate each other. A smile means acceptance and understanding which all children need and are you that person?

CPSIA information can be obtained
at www.ICGtesting.com
Printed in the USA
FSHW010510241219
65426FS